DESIGN SOURCES
FOR
SYMBOLISM

Jan Messent

Contents

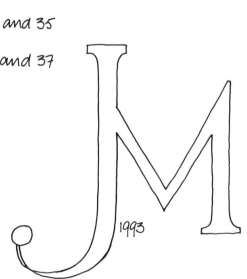

JM 1993

Glossary.

Allegory : a story or picture in which the characters or scenes convey a deeper meaning than the one shown "on the surface".

Attribute: the symbols bestowed upon a person by general consent become that person's attributes.

Cypher / Monogram: a combination of interlinked or interlaced letters (usually initials) such as Æ, M or M. Often used as logos.

Emblem: a device adopted by a person, family, firm, etc. as its own symbol. Logos and heraldic devices come into this category.

Icon: an image (usually a painting of a holy person) which has been imbued with the qualities of that person and which may now "stand in" as that person's representative.

Iconography is now a generally used term referring to a group of symbolic images which conveys more than one symbol alone would.

To "explain the iconography" means to discuss the meaning and relevance of all the symbols noted and recognised in the group. For instance, Jan van Eyck's "Arnolfini Wedding" is full of symbols, but there is much argument about their relevance to the scene.

Logo : short for logogram or logotype. Takes the form of an abbreviation of, or derivation from the full name (family or firm, etc.), known in the publicity business as "the heraldry of commerce". Some logos take the form of pictures which represent the name, e.g. "Greengate".

Sign: may be a sound or signal which evokes a response: a mark or gesture of some kind which we instantly recognise as information.

Symbol:

a. anything which may be regarded as a visual metaphor, simile or analogy to an idea or emotion, e.g. the moon sailing on a sea of stormy clouds.

b. Representation of a real thing, e.g. a house, flower, heart, in a highly stylised and simplified form. Over centuries of use, some forms have become abstract.

c. Fantastic or imaginary representation e.g. dragon, unicorn, of some real thing such as power, anger, strength, etc..

d. Personification of some virtue, thought or quality such as Wisdom, Beauty, Time, The Four Seasons.

e. Traditional and/or psychological system of endowing personal images with particular attributes. These may be archetypal forms passed on from earliest times which embody the spiritual qualities of, for example, the universe, life, male/female, etc. as circles, squares, triangles. It would be almost impossible now to invent an archetype as these rely for their effectiveness on our familiarity with them. Closely related to f.

f. Lines and shapes which suggest certain feelings of an abstract nature, e.g. leaning, falling, enclosing, pushing, flowing. These are much used by artists and designers to involve the viewer in some positive reaction, and are symbols belonging to a deeply inbuilt set of responses.

g. Joint symbols occur when two or more symbols are linked, sometimes quite un-naturally to convey a specific message,

e.g. both our hearts are pierced by love's arrow.

Symbols and symbolism can be found in roadsigns, trademarks, logos, badges, crests, emblems, tokens and favours, flags, heraldic devices, secret signs, passwords, codes, signals and beacons, etc., family, clan, kinship and tribal totems, numbers and letters, music and dance notation, written characters and alphabets, hieroglyphics, printing and publishing marks, punctuation, gestures, sign-language and mime, body-language, pageants and mystery plays, recurring motifs in written language and in music, metaphors and poetic imagery, zodiac signs, astronomy, astrology, chemistry, mathematics and all science subjects, religion and monarchy, clothes, regalia, trappings, badges of office, uniform, accessories and jewellery, amulets and talismans, flowers, plants, trees, etc., the animal kingdom and mythology.

For more symbolic connotations, look in any Thesaurus under the headings
INDICATION and SYMBOLS

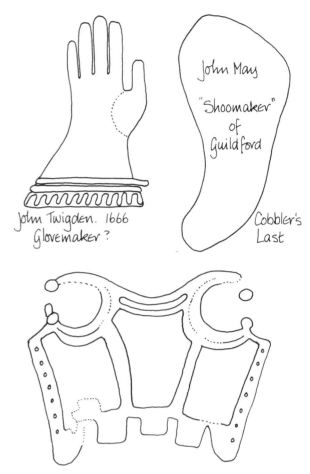

John Twigden. 1666
Glovemaker?

John May
"Shoomaker"
of
Guildford

Cobbler's
Last

Hugh Ley of Southwark. Staysmaker.

Tradesmen's Tokens of the 17th century show the symbol of each man's trade, as well as the name, date and value. The extreme simplicity of line reflects the fact that the device was impressed into lead and sometimes pewter, tin, silver and leather.

Mason's marks can still be found carved into the stonework of ancient buildings all over Europe. A mason who had completed his apprenticeship (a journeyman) would be given a symbol by his master which was based on that of his masonic lodge, though every mason's sign was different.

Postman

Wllm. Burnett of Chertsey.
Dairyman

Some of the masons' symbols at Bolton Priory, North Yorks, dating from 13th – 16th centuries.

Signs and Logos

Which way?   What will you find?   Who can go — and who can not go —   Be warned!

The National Trust uses the ancient oak leaf

English Heritage uses a building ground-plan.

The National Trust for Scotland has battlements resembling a crown, with St. Andrew's cross underneath.

Shell: a pictorial symbol based on the name alone.

The Timberland Company logo is more stylised than natural.

This is embossed on leather goods.

Volkswagen —

The initial letters of the company form a neat monogram.

A Japanese personal crest is rendered almost abstract.

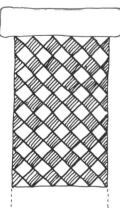

A chequered pattern painted on the doorposts was the customary sign of the tavern.

Inn sign: "The Golden Fleece" at Thirsk in North Yorks.

Inn rooms were often known by their symbols rather than by numbers. This one is from the "Sun Room" at the Royal Fountain in Sheerness.

<u>Widow's Quilt Patchwork</u>
pattern, also known as
"Darts of Death"
A most versatile motif which
symbolises death's dart, can
be turned to form blocks or
borders. To try out ideas, make
several units and cut them
out separately, then place
these in different formations.
The permutations are
numerous, especially when
counter-change tones are
also used as in the block of
repeats on the far right.

Pelt Patchwork / Siberia

The rough sketch on the left was made
from a B/W photograph of a PELT PATCH-
WORK made in Siberia. These 3-toned
patchworks are made from animal pelts
and this particular one is called
"Northern Lights" – a phenomenon which
must be familiar to families living in
Arctic regions. Patchwork clothes are joined
in places where the pattern will not necessarily
continue across, resulting in a "fractured"
effect, which I find particularly interesting.
This is what I have tried to make even more
obvious in the recreation of the design
below. Only the lower two-thirds of the
pattern have been drawn, but enough to
show that this symbolic design has great
potential in many different media.

snake
rectangular fields and seas moved by the wind

rain and ripples on sea

veins on coconut-leaf and grasses

dark corners indicate calm on deep waters
Design on a bamboo case from Melanesia

Despite the geometrical style of the designs on this page, they are all based on natural phenomena. They are expressed as symbols to show fields, lakes, mountains, clouds, footprints, etc., and each design takes on a specific meaning as soon as the name is revealed. In fact, more than one name and meaning is sometimes given to the same design depending on its connotations and on the geographical area. For instance, the patchwork pattern known as Wandering Foot was unpopular with wives who did not want it used on their quilts for fear of invoking a wanderlust in their husbands, nor were children allowed to sleep under such a quilt in case they should grow up to be restless and unsettled. Eventually, it was re-named Turkey Track or, when the motif was green on a white background, Iris Leaf.

Jacob's Ladder also goes under a variety of names depending on the state where it was being made. In Kentucky, it became known as Underground Railroad, which meant the secret escape routes by which slaves made their way to Canada.

mountains   sunshine
green grass

sand and sunlight

timber-covered mountains

red ground

lake with inlet

green trees

Parfleche design : Shoshone Indian

Moon over the Mountain Patchwork

Flying Clouds Patchwork

Wandering Foot also known as Turkey Track

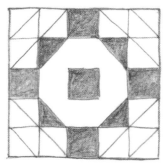

Goose in the Pond

Jacob's Ladder (Iowa Amish)

MAN

Man is often represented as the sun and the power of the heavens. (See also page 38)
The four winds are often seen as men.
Representing the whole man, his face can be seen inside the sun's disc in early painted manuscripts and on old tiles.
Phallic symbols abound in pre-history, especially as carved stones and reliefs representing the generative forces of nature.
Louis IVX of France was known to his people as the Sun King, and the Peruvian Inca was venerated as the son of the sun. (See page 11.)

Old Father Time symbolises mortality : he carries a scythe and an hour-glass.
The Green Man is of ancient origin : depictions of him can be seen all over Europe in stone, wood and metal, dating from earliest times to the present day. He symbolises renewal, regeneration, immortality, and is usually seen with foliage issuing from his mouth and surrounding his head. (See page 28)

WOMAN

Symbolically, probably more interesting than man, she is known as the Earth Mother and the Great Goddess for her obvious links to the powers of reproduction and the life-giving forces of nature, regeneration (i.e. the seasons) and protection.
Woman's other main symbol is the moon, particularly the crescent moon, its light and the stars. Diana was the moon-goddess, huntress of the sky.
Her other representations are more complex and depend on the mythology and tradition of the various countries. Not all is benign or creative, it can also be dark and destructive, often being seen as the opposite of the positive male aspect.

Dual symbol : the yin-yang is a well-known symbol of ancient Chinese origin which represents the duality and complementary opposites of all forms of life, powers and qualities, not only male and female.

KING AND QUEEN

Together, the king and queen represent perfect union as two halves of the whole.
They are often shown as the sun and moon, heaven and earth, day and night, gold and silver. The king's attributes are the sun, a crown of golden rays, sceptre, orb, sword, arrows and throne. Named kings usually hold their own symbols or attributes.

The queen is the Queen of Heaven or the Great Mother. She wears a crown of stars, and a blue mantle to symbolise the sky. Her attributes are the crescent moon, stars, orb, sceptre and chalice.
Examples : The Queen of the Night, from Mozart's "The Magic Flute".
　　　　　Queen of the May : the spirit of springtime and renewal.
　　　　　Queen of Hearts : nursery rhyme, playing cards, Alice in Wonderland.
　　　　　Queen of Spades : symbolises death.
　　　　　The Snow/Ice Queen : symbolises frozen emotions. Oscar Wilde's story.

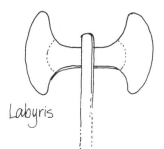

Labyris

The double-headed axe is a symbol of feminists, denoting unity and strength.

The ancient female symbol is also that of Venus, goddess of love.

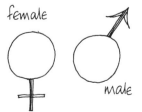

female

male

The story of the Garden of Eden can be used to illustrate the use of body language (i.e. symbolic gestures) re-enforced by symbols to explain the scene more fully.

1. Before the fall (left): Upright "open" body. Adam has palms up and arms outspread to signify acceptance and agreement.

2. After the fall: bent "closed" body, faces, heads and nakedness covered to signify shame. Eyes closed against the terrible angel.

3. Angel: commanding position, head held high. Arm and hand signify dismissal.

4. Symbols: Tree of Knowledge and forbidden fruit
Evil serpent
Garden: peace and happiness
Sun: light and goodness.   Moon: darkness, despair
Angel: messenger from God, with sword of authority.
(Halo — holiness, wings — supernatural being.)

Horizontal lines (mountains and river) help to counter-balance the vertical lines of figures and tree. The wide-spread branches of the tree also have the same effect.
The tree trunk conveniently divides the scene into "before and after".

The hand has always been a universal symbol with endless powers of expression and meaning from praise to submission, friendship to enmity and speech to silence. The hands painted on walls of caves in prehistoric times testify to its significance as a powerful symbol of prayer and life. The right hand (dexter) is known as the seat of power and the left hand (sinister) as the seat of receptivity. Hands placed palm to palm now mean prayer or supplication, but in earlier times the praying attitude was with the hands held apart and palms facing forwards.

The head symbolises the life-force, or genius, of the person, but in design is often found to represent the complete body of a man or woman. Dual and triple heads represent multiple powers of spirituality, also the past, present and future as with Janus (above) who was the Roman god of doorways and entrances after whom the month of January was named. He had the power to look both backwards and forwards, towards the old and the new, beginnings and endings, destiny, departure and return, etc..

Janus

The eye is a massively complex symbol used to represent good as well as evil things. Some of its meanings are enlightenment, knowledge, intuitive vision and vigilance. In early times, the "evil eye" used to have special powers. The Eye of Horus is seen extensively in wall-paintings of ancient Egypt and has special significance, Horus being one of the names of the sun god.

Mask with eyebrows symbolising the squid.
Tlingit – North America

The mask is a useful symbol with many meanings, representing, among other things, the hidden part of one's personality, the adopted nature of something else or some identifying character. It can also be used to adopt the wisdom or attributes of animals and birds (see left). Masks can be comic, tragic or god-like.

The skull was a favourite Victorian symbol of mourning. Generally, it denotes death, the moon, the dying sun (i.e. the transitory nature of life) and, with the skeleton, symbolises the swift passage of time and therefore life. The skeleton is sometimes used as the figure of Old Father Time.

Arms, upraised, denote supplication, prayer, and surrender. They have many other symbolic meanings worthy of detailed research, especially in the Christian church.

Feet symbolise freedom of movement. Washing and kissing the feet symbolises humility. Footprints are a symbol of the divine presence; those going in opposite directions denote past and present (or future) as well as coming and going.

Shaman's Deer mask.

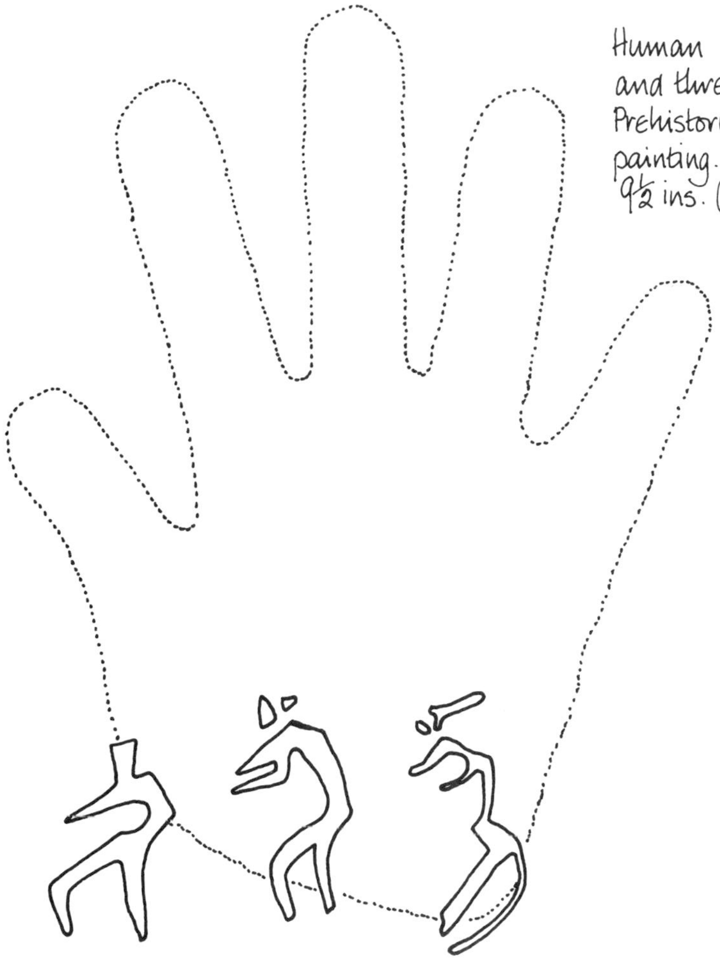

Human hand
and three figures.
Prehistoric rock
painting. Libya.
9½ ins. (24cms.)

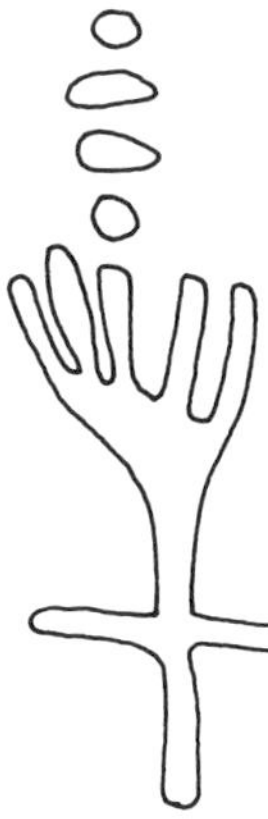

Outstretched hand,
from a rock
painting of
neolithic times.
Scandinavia

Could this have
been a request
for rain or
crops?

An ancient Syrian
in a symbolic
attitude of
supplication, from
a wall-painting
of ancient Egypt.

Bottom left: a mask of
gold made by the Incas of
ancient Peru represents
the sun in the same way
as that seen on Louis XIV's
theatrical costume (right).

Bottom right: the eye of
Horus, sun god of ancient Egypt,
also known as the wedjat eye.

The emblem of the Sun King from the
costume of Louis XIV as
Le Roi Soleil.

Sun tile of ancient origin.

11.

Garments

Crown : an important symbol of various meanings depending on the context.
Variously, it can mean sovereignty, victory, the circle of time and continuity, energy and power: the points of the crown may symbolise the sun's rays.
The crown of thorns portrays the passion of Christ, and crowns of laurels, parsley, pine, wild olives, flowers, roses and ears of corn are known in ancient mythology.

Hat : symbol of authority and power. "Changing hats" denotes a change of opinions, attitudes or occupations, since the head is the receptacle of thoughts.
Hat shapes depict social orders and occupations.
Hat removal and bare-headedness denote respect, but only in some parts of the world.

Veil : a highly symbolic garment variously denoting darkness, hiding, inscrutability and secrecy, ignorance and mourning. It can also indicate protection, submission, modesty and chastity.
Used by Puccini's "Turandot" as a protection and
by Salome as a means of revelation, as in a ceremonial unveiling of something special.

Hood : this has a similar significance, suggesting invisibility and withdrawal, as with the covering of the sun in autumn.

Mantle or Cloak : similar in meaning to the veil and hood, though the cloak also bestows a certain dignity and disguise.
A magic cloak or mantle is usually invisible and may also suggest transformation, as in "wearing the mantle of wisdom and beauty."

Robe : though similar in function to the mantle and cloak, the robe appears to have an altogether more positive symbolism, especially the shape of the individual garments, the sleeves, seams, lower edges and decoration. This garment's potential should be fully explored, as the robe itself can carry an abundance of other symbols.

Shoes : much symbolism, both as a sign of freedom and of possession.
Shoes have often been sealed into the chimney-piece of houses to ward off evil spirits, and are still used as part of the wedding symbolism to signify the husband's acceptance of the wife as his property. !

Gloves : "hand-in-glove" signifies a close collaboration,
"to throw down the glove" is an ancient form of challenge.
The white glove, worn by judges and priests, signifies purity, and is also worn by policemen whose signals need to be seen. The iron glove indicates firmness and inflexibility.

Fan : has significance both in shape and in use. The typical fan shape can be said to represent life itself, beginning at the point and widening out as the experience of life does. The folding fan depicts changes in the aspects of the moon, and this in turn is associated with feminine changeability. Its fluttering action represents movements of the air and thus the spirit in all its forms.

Umbrella and Parasol : visually, it has connections with the wheel and the solar disc, so not surprisingly its symbolism is related to the canopy of the heavens, the shelter of the branches of the cosmic tree and protection in general. It can also be seen as the sun's rays with the world axis as its haft.

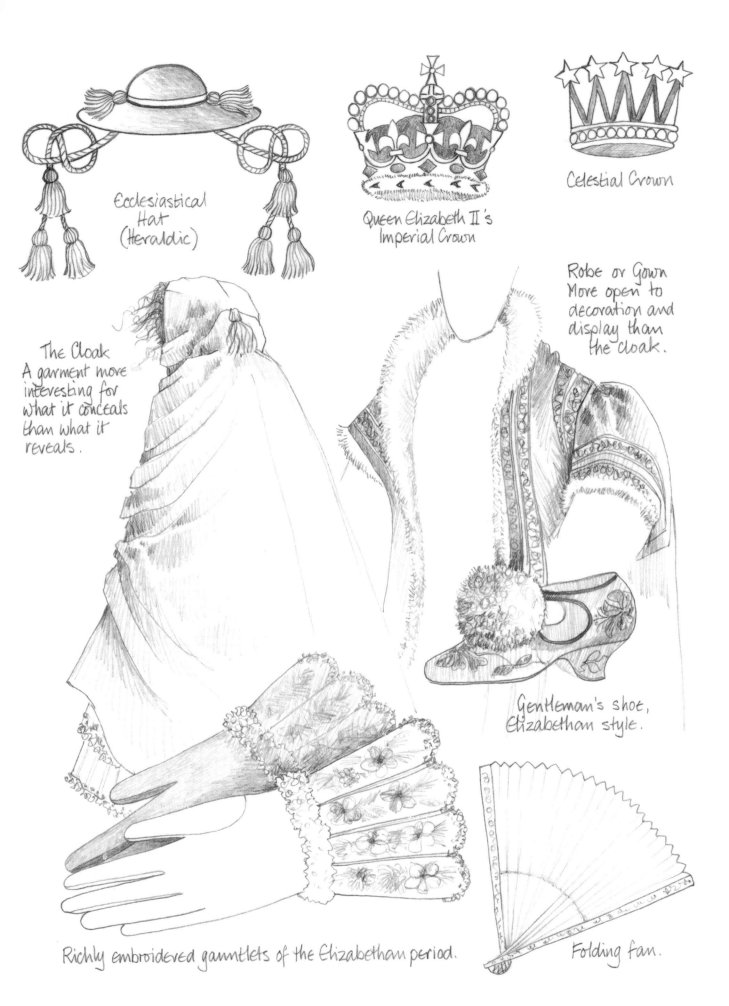

Ecclesiastical
Hat
(Heraldic)

Queen Elizabeth II's
Imperial Crown

Celestial Crown

The Cloak
A garment more
interesting for
what it conceals
than what it
reveals.

Robe or Gown
More open to
decoration and
display than
the cloak.

Gentleman's shoe,
Elizabethan style.

Richly embroidered gauntlets of the Elizabethan period.

Folding fan.

13

The Tree of Jesse

The diagram opposite symbolises the genealogical descent of Christ from Jesse, the father of David, as prophesied by Isaiah (ch.11, v.1) "And there shall come forth a rod out of the stem of Jesse, and a branch shall grow out of his roots." This concept has been illustrated for centuries in many ways and in many media. It can most often be seen in ecclesiastical embroidery of the medieval period, in stained glass windows and in tapestries. Traditionally, the tree is a vine, though this varies, and is usually treated in a stylised manner.

The Kings of Judah form the trunk of the tree (i.e. David, Solomon, etc.) with the prophets who proclaimed the coming of the Messiah on the side branches. Moses is sometimes seen too, bearing the law-giving tablets. Jesse lies in repose at the base and at the apex is usually either the Virgin and Child, the Nativity or Christ alone. Doves, representing the Holy Spirit, are here seen on either side.

The Star of David is a symbol of the Jewish faith. It depicts the Creation and is also known as the Seal of Solomon.

The Menorah, or seven-branched candlestick is another Jewish symbol indicating the divine presence. The seven branches symbolise, among other things, the seven days of the week. The Menorah is a powerful symbol of hope.

The cross is a universal symbol with countless meanings and, with the circle, is probably the oldest one in the world. To Christians, it symbolises salvation through Christ's sacrifice. The Y cross on the priest's chasuble represents Christ's arms extended on the cross, and the "lifting up of hands" in prayer.

Chalice : a symbol of the blood of Christ and the cup of salvation.

See page 16 for these four symbols.

Chi-Rho : adopted by Christians from an ancient symbol as the first two letters of Christ's name.

Ankh : an ancient Egyptian symbol of life, the universe, the key of knowledge.

Tau : denotes life and supreme power. It is also a phallic symbol. As a hammer, it is an attribute of the thunder god.

Cherub

This decorated initial letter from a late 12th century manuscript symbolises the domination of the church over kingship.
The bishop, wearing the mitre, halo, and holding a hand in blessing, holds the sacred law above the king (with crown and sword) in a clear illustration of the position.

Seraph. (See also page 17)

15

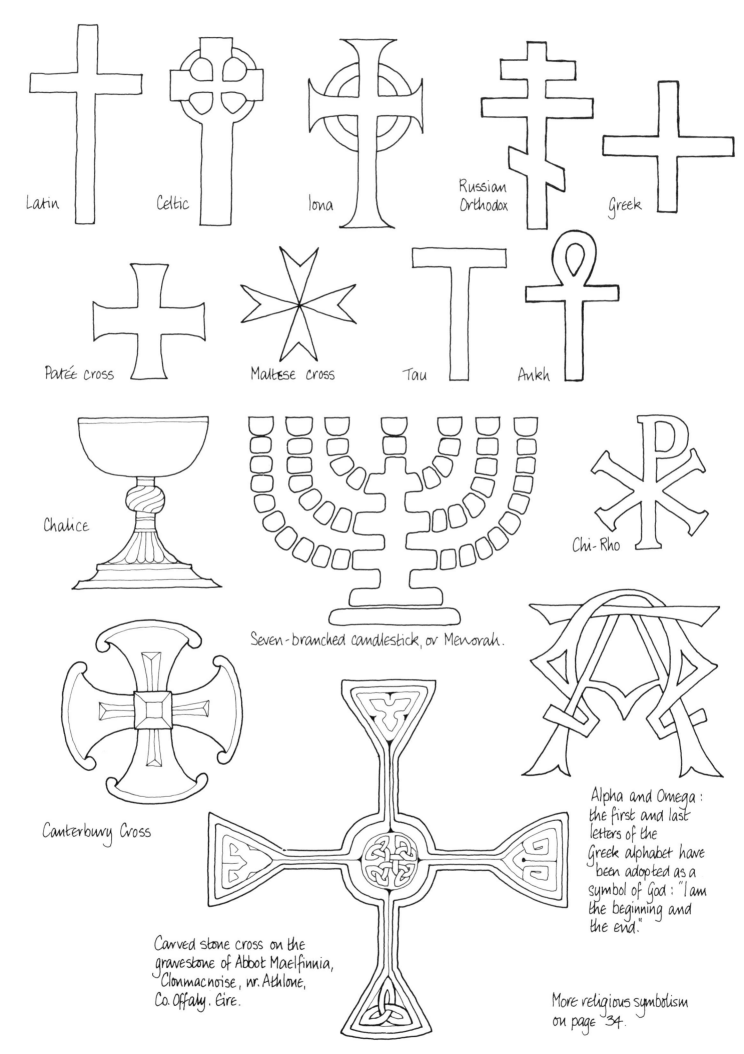

Latin

Celtic

Iona

Russian Orthodox

Greek

Patée cross

Maltese cross

Tau

Ankh

Chalice

Seven-branched candlestick, or Menorah.

Chi-Rho

Canterbury Cross

Carved stone cross on the gravestone of Abbot Maelfinnia, Clonmacnoise, nr. Athlone, Co. Offaly. Éire.

Alpha and Omega: the first and last letters of the Greek alphabet have been adopted as a symbol of God: "I am the beginning and the end."

More religious symbolism on page 34.

Detail:

showing one of
Christ's disciples from an embroidered
altar-frontal of 1315-35.

Detail

from a stained glass window
by Edward Burne-Jones, c. 1880

Haloes are a symbol of divinity: they may be luminous or transparent, plain or decorated, behind the head of the divine one, or above it. Sometimes the halo is seen as a solid disc, like a gold plate, or it may consist of bright rays of light in a circular or star-shaped formation.

Angels are messengers of God, and powers of the invisible world. They are represented in many religions.
Some are shown with six wings, some with four, and others with only two, these varying greatly in style as can be seen here.
See also page 14

Left: a six-winged
seraph, from an
Armenian
stone-carving.

Right: an angel with most
unusual wings from the Easter
Hanging, Lüene Convent,
Germany, 1504-5

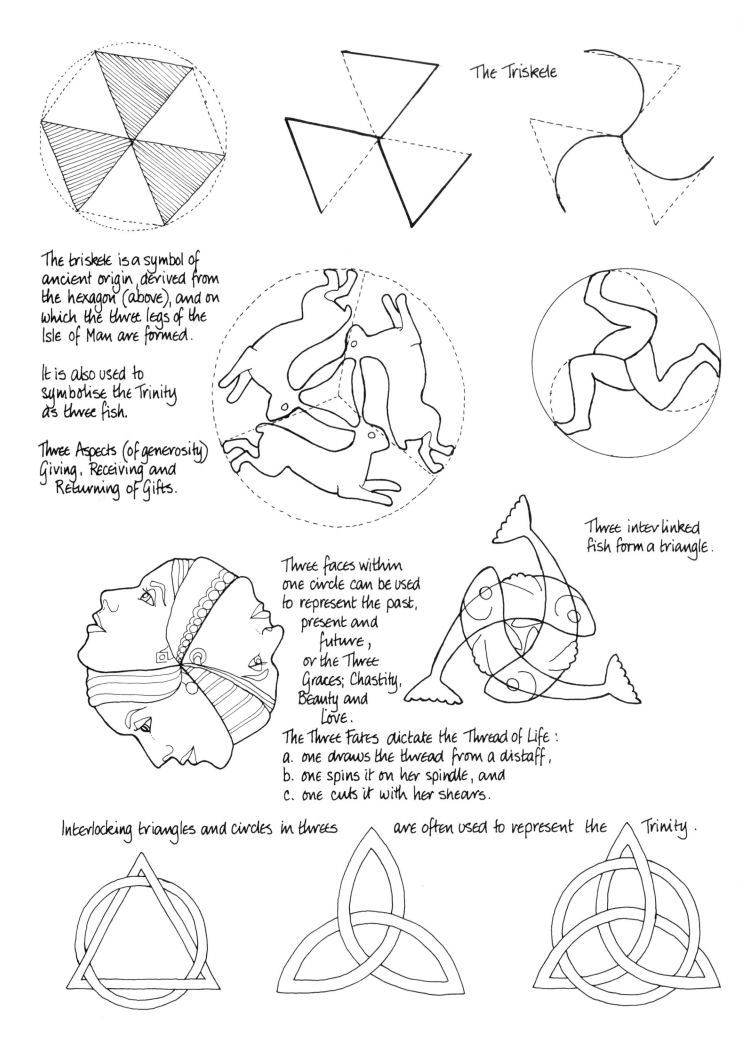

The Triskele

The triskele is a symbol of ancient origin, derived from the hexagon (above), and on which the three legs of the Isle of Man are formed.

It is also used to symbolise the Trinity as three fish.

Three Aspects (of generosity) Giving, Receiving and Returning of Gifts.

Three interlinked fish form a triangle.

Three faces within one circle can be used to represent the past, present and future, or the Three Graces; Chastity, Beauty and Love.

The Three Fates dictate the Thread of Life :
a. one draws the thread from a distaff,
b. one spins it on her spindle, and
c. one cuts it with her shears.

Interlocking triangles and circles in threes   are often used to represent the   Trinity.

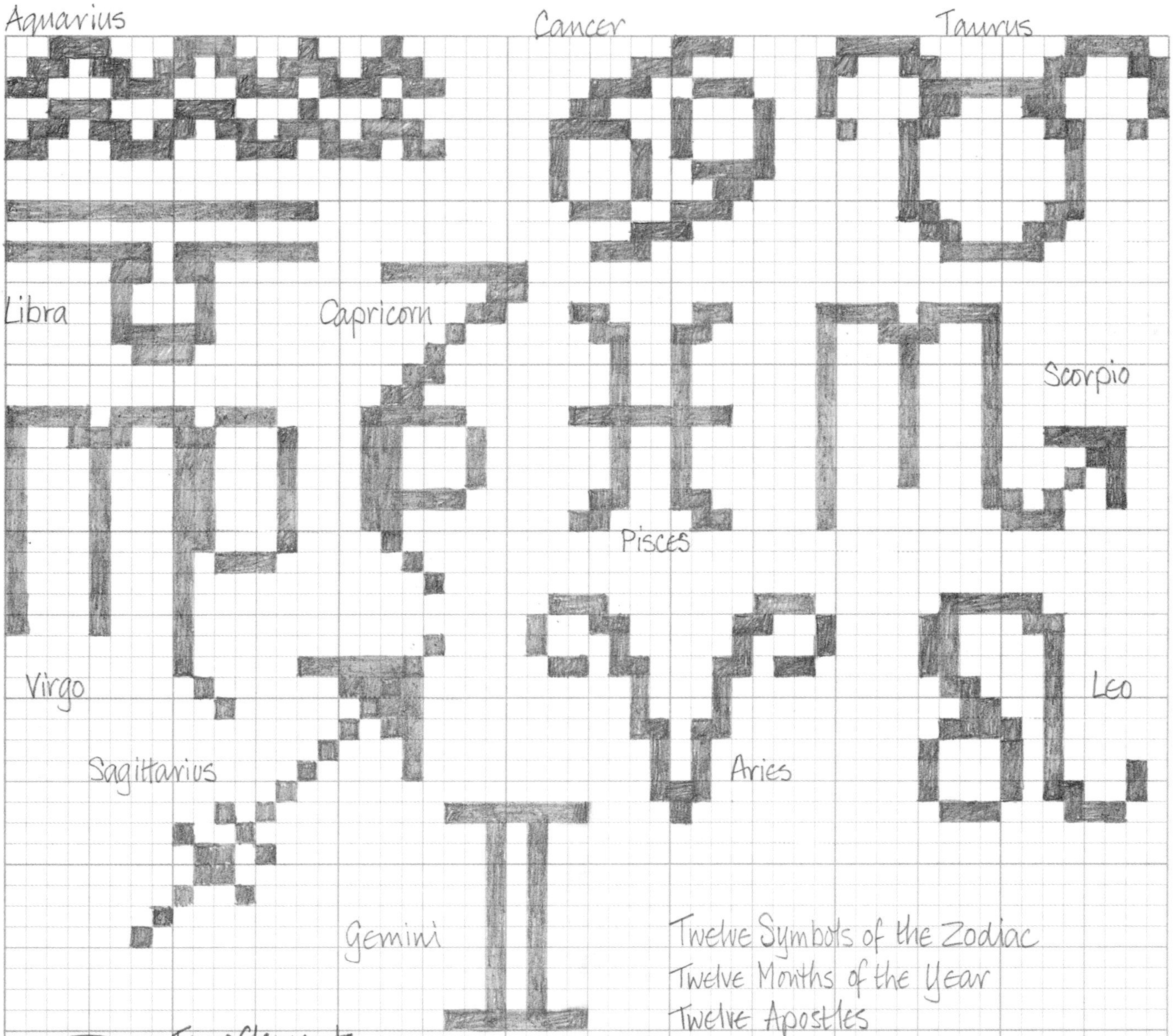

Aquarius

Cancer

Taurus

Libra

Capricorn

Scorpio

Pisces

Virgo

Leo

Sagittarius

Aries

Gemini

Twelve Symbols of the Zodiac
Twelve Months of the Year
Twelve Apostles

Four Elements

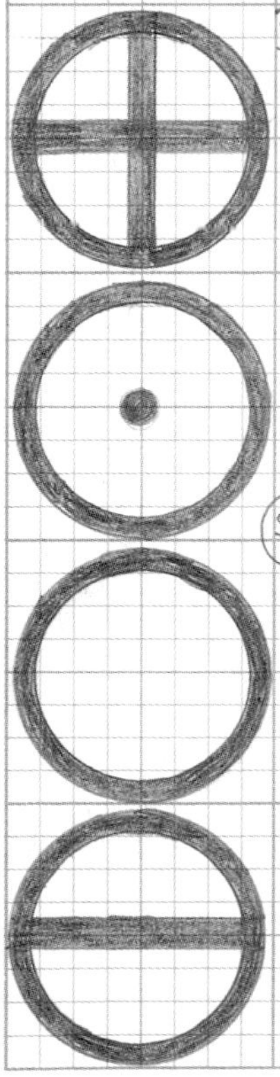

Earth   Four Ages of Man — infant, youth, maturity, old age.

          Four Seasons — spring, summer, autumn, winter

Air   Five Senses — hearing / musical instrument
                        sight / mirror
(see also page 38)   taste / basket of fruit
                        smell / flowers, or vase of perfume
Fire   touch / hedgehog, ermine or bird on the hand.

          Six Works of Mercy — tending the hungry, thirsty,
                        stranger, naked, sick, prisoner.

Water   Seven Days of the Week

          Seven Stars of the Pleiades (seven sisters)

Earth / World / Life / Death

World symbols have been used throughout the world to express the power of the earth and the meaning of the universe. Sometimes they signify one aspect only, sometimes many, but one of the oldest and most often seen is that of the Earth Mother. She is represented as a voluptuous fertile figure denoting the fecundity of nature, renewal and regeneration of life. The well-known corn-dolly is a device which represents the spirit of the corn which must be preserved at the end of the harvest in order to facilitate the growth of the new seed in the next growing season.

Other symbols of the world and nature include
The Four Elements and the Seasons
Mountains
Sun and Moon, planets
Rainbow, dawn and twilight
Rivers, water, fountains, wells and whirlpools
Mirror and reflections
Fire, flame, candle, lamp and torch
Labrynth and maze

The Circle:
probably the oldest known symbol of all time. Concentric circles are more or less bound up with the movement of the stars and planets, especially the sun and moon, symbols of power, life and death. Many rituals take the form of circles, initiation dances, fertility and celebration dances encircling stones and trees (as in the maypole dance).
Fairy toadstool rings.
Mandalas: evoking wheels and machinery, originated in Afghanistan, Tibet and Japan and are used as an aid to meditation.
The crescent, the ring and the spiral are also significant in depicting various aspects of life.

Also significant are the square, cube, star, lozenge, pentagram, octagon, triangle, zig-zag, swastika, and many other shapes which enclose.

Right: the Minoan Great Mother holding a double-headed axe in each hand as a symbol of power.

Far right: a terracotta figurine of a Mother Goddess from Mohenjo-Daro, India.

The ancient symbol of the universe: the centre signifies the earth, the inner ring the oceans, and the outer ring the heavens.

solar signs

Dance in a Ring

Tiny symbols of Life form the centres of each motif on this embroidery from Turkmenistan.

Not surprisingly, the most common, important, and diverse symbols of all, and the most ancient, are those concerning aspects of life and death. Though this subject will never cease to hold an important position in our thinking, it was even more to the fore in the minds of our ancestors, as it is still to societies who live closer to nature than we do. The plaintive symbolism with which we have become so familiar is as relevant now as it was in earliest times when men drew sun-discs on the walls of caves. The forces of nature, the elements, the pattern of our lives has not changed. It would now be almost impossible to invent new and more meaningful symbols than those which already exist; indeed, their simple primitive quality is what speaks to us most clearly. But we can re-use and re-connect them to our own designs knowing that they will be recognised and understood by most people without the need for laborious explanations. This is not to say, of course, that one cannot add other personal elements; these extras are what will give meaning to a design on a more intimate level.

Above: From a Chinese painting, an old sage hands a peach to an excited child. The peach is a symbol of longevity.

Life: Symbols of long life are often those things which are noted for the same quality, the oak tree, the vine, mountains, gemstones, stars, etc.. Also those creatures like the butterfly which pass through the larval and chrysalis stages to reach maturity. Frogs and fish too are significant.
   The Tree of Life (see p.29) is also one of the best known life symbols, as are the fungus and many fruits.

Death: the King of Death is often depicted as a skeleton, dressed as Old Father Time, or walking with him. He may hold a sword, scythe, sickle or hour-glass. Other symbols of death are the skull, veil, serpent, scorpion, ashes, dead flowers, coffins and tombstones.

Specially-designed mourning jewellery has existed for many centuries and became particularly popular in Victorian times. This would take the form of rings, lockets, pendants and brooches containing inscriptions, plaited hair, portraits or other personal mementos of the deceased. Black fans were indicative of mourning, as were black clothes (in the western world), black armbands for men (19th C.) or, earlier, a knot of black ribbons attached to an armband. Earlier still, in the 17th. C., bands of willow were worn round the hat, and ladies carried posies of rosemary,
   (for remembrance).

Amulets and talismans appear to take various forms: as a protection against evil, sickness and accident, as an aid to reach heavenly status after death, as a means of absorbing the powers of particular animals, as an aid to healing or bodily functions such as walking, or spiritual powers such as wisdom or courage, as a bringer of fertility and an aid to childbirth, and also as a bringer of good fortune generally.

In ancient Egypt, most jewellery had a magical significance. Amulets were more effective when worn near the heart (collars, pendants, etc.). Cylindrical and box-shaped amulets of metal containing magic charms written on papyrus were worn round the neck.

The ancient Chinese regarded jade as an especially potent source of magical and spiritual qualities. Jade jewellery was worn from earliest times to protect the wearers against evil.

Early Christians often wore amulets containing the Chi-Rho monogram and the X (an ancient symbol of protection) not only as an identification but also as a protection against ill-fortune.

In Anglo-Saxon times, runic inscriptions were inscribed on amuletic jewellery as a protection against evil, as were religious inscriptions on pendants worn by pilgrims to holy shrines. The names of Jesus and the three kings were thought to have been a protection against epilepsy.

The pineapple is thought to bring good fortune, to bring friends closer together, hospitality and fertility. (Quite a potent mixture!)

Rock-crystal was commonly believed, in antiquity and medieval times, to have amuletic properties and to ensure a plentiful supply of milk after childbirth.
Blue lapis lazuli symbolised the colour of the heavens.
Red carnelian was the colour of life-blood.
Green feldspar, or turquoise, was the colour of new life.

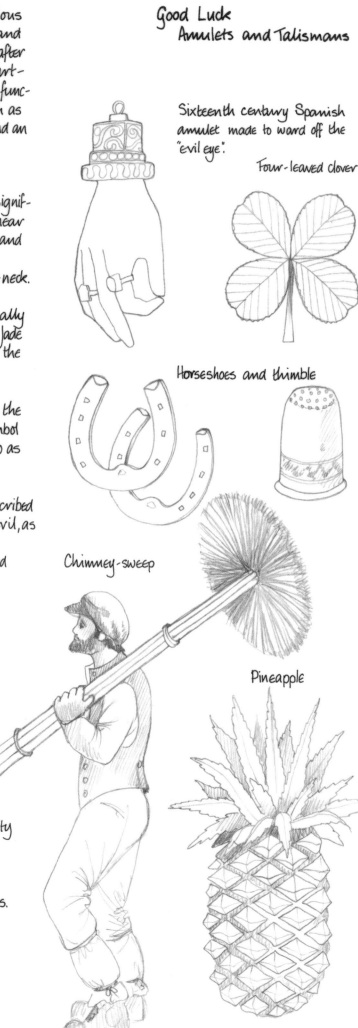

Good Luck
Amulets and Talismans

Sixteenth century Spanish amulet made to ward off the "evil eye".

Four-leaved clover

Horseshoes and thimble

Chimney-sweep

Pineapple

22

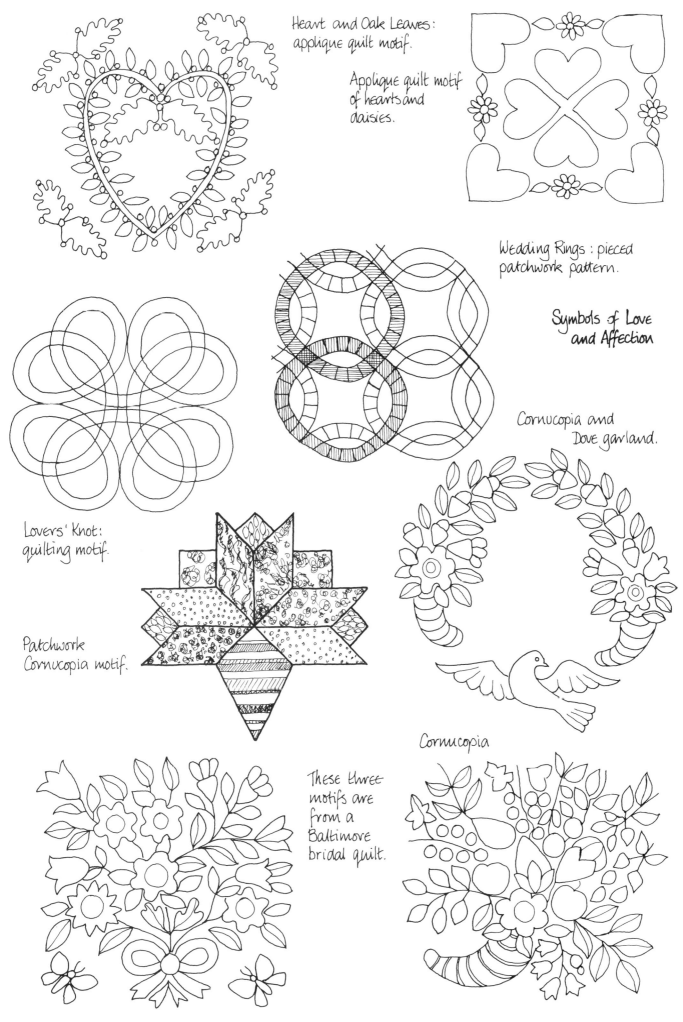

Heart and Oak Leaves: applique quilt motif.

Applique quilt motif of hearts and daisies.

Wedding Rings : pieced patchwork pattern.

Symbols of Love and Affection

Cornucopia and Dove garland.

Lovers' Knot: quilting motif.

Patchwork Cornucopia motif.

Cornucopia

These three motifs are from a Baltimore bridal quilt.

23

Symbols of Love and Affection

Cupid and cherubs
Hearts
Gemstones
Rings
Clasped hands
Turtle doves (Love birds)
Anchor
Shoe
Welsh love spoons
Bells

MDI
18 56

24

Symbols of Love and Affection

Cupid: he was the boy-god of love, son of Venus, Goddess of Love.
  A Roman adaptation of the Greek Eros.

Cherubs: in this context, tiny angels: actually cherubim. Protective.

Heart: the centre of all emotions, particularly of love and affection. A universal symbol.

Gemstones: always thought to have magical powers, they have many meanings to those who love.
  Huge amount of symbolism attached to every type. Research recommended.

Rings: can be seen as symbols of the cycle of life, continuity, eternity, etc..

Clasped hands: universal symbol of a pledge, promise, joining together, etc..

Turtle Dove: came to be known as "love-birds" for their affectionate "billing and coo-ing".
  Dove represents simplicity, innocence and purity, and is the messenger of love.

Anchor: means hope, steadfastness, stability, tranquility, safety and security.

Shoe: symbolises the possession of the bride by the bridegroom.   (Not for throwing !)

Love-spoons: the one shown is from the Welsh Folk Museum, St.Fagans. Other love-tokens (worldwide)
  include carved knitting-sheaths, combs, lace-bobbins, rolling-pins, etc.. Also pin-cushions
  and Valentine cards.   A good area for research.

Bells: represent joy and good news.

Cornucopia: a curved horn-shaped vessel (with phallic connotations) also known as the Horn of Plenty.
  Always shown full of fruit, flowers, etc., it symbolises abundance, fertility and fruitfulness.
  Favourite symbol on American bridal quilts of the 19th C. (See page 23.)

Oak leaves: strength, steadfastness and longevity.   (See page 31.)

Lovers' Knot: has no ends, therefore can never be untied.   Knots are significant to many countries.

Other symbols may include good-luck tokens and those associated with life, longevity, fecundity,
hospitality, peace, etc.. For a comprehensive and detailed description of all things to do with this
subject, see "Love and Marriage" by Christine Bloxham and Molly Picken, published by
Webb and Bower (1990) ISBN 0.86350.336.5

Flowers which symbolise Love and Affection are many and varied ; they include

Rose: love (Dog-rose — pleasure and pain)
Forget-me-not: true love
Bay: constancy
Carnation (pink): woman's love
Honeysuckle: generosity and devotion
Ivy: friendship and fidelity
Myrtle: love
Rosemary: remembrance
Tulip (red): a declaration of love
Orange blossom: chastity

Many other flowers and plants have a
complex symbolism to do with love,
differently coloured roses mean a variety
of things and trees also have significance.
It is a huge area for research tied up with
ancient folk-lore and tradition, all of
which vary from one country to another.

Below: Chronicles of Courtly Love from Regensburg, c.1390.
Details of three roundels from a large tapestry show hilarious
scenes of a symbolic nature.

Rosemary

Carnation /pink

Tulip

Bay

Myrtle

Dog-Rose

Honeysuckle

Forget-me-not

Flowers of Love and Affection.

Symbolism described on
previous page. See also page 36.

Ivy

Design based on a watercolour painting of "Wild Roses" by Charlotte Brontë, dated 1830. These fragrant five-petalled flowers, found in the local hedgerows, are very pale pink, shading to white in the centre. The original painting is in the Brontë Museum, Haworth, North Yorkshire.

Roses
the flowers of Love.

Rose Garland
from a Baltimore Quilt
Red and deep green.

Square "Wild Rose" motif.

The Tudor Rose was adopted as the emblem of the Royal House of Tudor when Henry VII, father of Henry VIII, married Elizabeth of York, thus helping to resolve the differences between the two warring houses of Lancaster and York, whose emblems were (and still are) the red and white roses, respectively.

The outer rose is bright red and the inner one is white.

"Wreath of Roses", applique quilt motif.

27

TREES

Including the universal Tree of Life, trees generally have an immense symbolic significance world-wide. Their longevity, their contact with the deeper parts of the earth, the world centre, the waters and the heavens are aspects which have relevance to human lives and these have been recognised since ancient times. Their fruits and various peculiarities are further elements in their veneration as magical and sacred objects. Even twisted and deformed specimens have their powers, it seems. There is something decidedly feminine in the nourishing, protecting and supporting role played by trees in life, though European folk traditions still make annual reference to such characters as the Green Man, Robin Hood, and Jack in the Green.

One way or another, magical significance can be attached to almost all types of tree, but below are just some of the most familiar ones. All fruit-bearing trees are, to some extent, sacred, especially the apple, pear, plum, vine, date, fig, olive, almond, peach, mulberry and elderberry.

Mistletoe, clinging to the bare branches of the oak-tree is a symbol of life's continuity.

Hawthorn: covered with flowers in spring, leaves in summer, berries in autumn/winter. Considered to be sheltered (and therefore a barrier) against evil.

Apple: the tree in the Garden of Eden (The Tree of Knowledge) was thought to have been an apple tree. In ancient religions, the apple was highly prized as an emblem of the renewal of youth.

Ash: the Great Earth Tree, Yggdrasil of Norse mythology, was thought to be an ash tree. It holds up the heavens and has its roots in hell.

Elder: (sambucus niger) called the magic Trammon Tree in the Isle of Man. A sacred tree which should not be uprooted or cut without its permission. (The berries are wonderful in pies, but always thank the tree after picking.)

Yew: because of the great age to which these trees live, they are thought to have special links with the past. Still a sacred tree, they are often found in churchyards.

Rowan, or Mountain Ash: has symbolic significance in the Scottish Highlands.

Other trees in this category include the acacia, acanthus, aspen, birch, cedar, cypress, pine, witchhazel, laurel, willow, olive, palm, myrtle and bay.

The Green Man carved on a wooden panel in the church at Sampford Courtney, Devon in the 15th century.

This mythological figure is well represented in countless buildings, both religious and secular, all over Europe from earliest times to the present day. He is always depicted with foliage issuing from his mouth, symbolising the regeneration and renewal of life throughout the seasons, dying in winter only to be reborn each spring. Although pagan in origin, this concept is not seen to be out of place in Christian settings. He is an example of the close association between nature and religious beliefs.

A white cotton prayer mat, embroidered in Afghanistan bears a highly stylised Tree of Life motif in the centre of two hands (not shown).

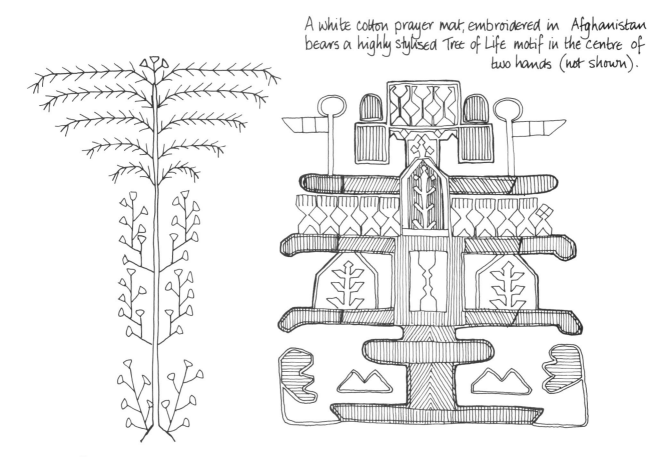

Tree of Life motif from an oriental carpet.

The Tree of Life symbol is of very ancient origin and is found world-wide in a variety of media, stone and wood-carving, paintings, embroidery, weaving and stained glass. It takes on a variety of forms too, sometimes abstract, always highly stylised and sometimes semi-naturalistic.

It represents the structure of the universe in that its roots are the dark underworld, the trunk is life itself and its branches are the vault of heaven.

The traditional maypole is a remnant of pagan tree-worship during which a dance round the sacred tree was expected to promote good crops at the beginning of the growing season.

The mulberry tree is the Chinese Tree of Life, and in some Persian carpets, the Tree of Life appears as a cypress which, as an evergreen, represents everlasting life, undying spirit, immortality. A deciduous tree is the world in constant renewal and regeneration, dying to live, resurrection, reproduction: the life principal. This concept is also represented in the symbolism of the Green Man whose effigy has been carved in many buildings in Europe since earliest times.

Woven Tree of Life motif from Sweden. 1781

The weeping willow is a symbol of sorrow and death.

Embroidered Apple Tree.
Designed by May Morris, late 19th C.

Fruit Trees, in general, symbolise immortality. More particularly, but still over-simplified, meanings are as follows:

Lemon: a Christian symbol of faithfulness in love.
Pear: hope and good health
Apple: fertility, love, joyousness, knowledge, wisdom, etc.
Plum: longevity. Christian symbol of independence and fidelity
Cherry: Christian symbol of the fruit of Paradise, blessedness, sweetness, etc.

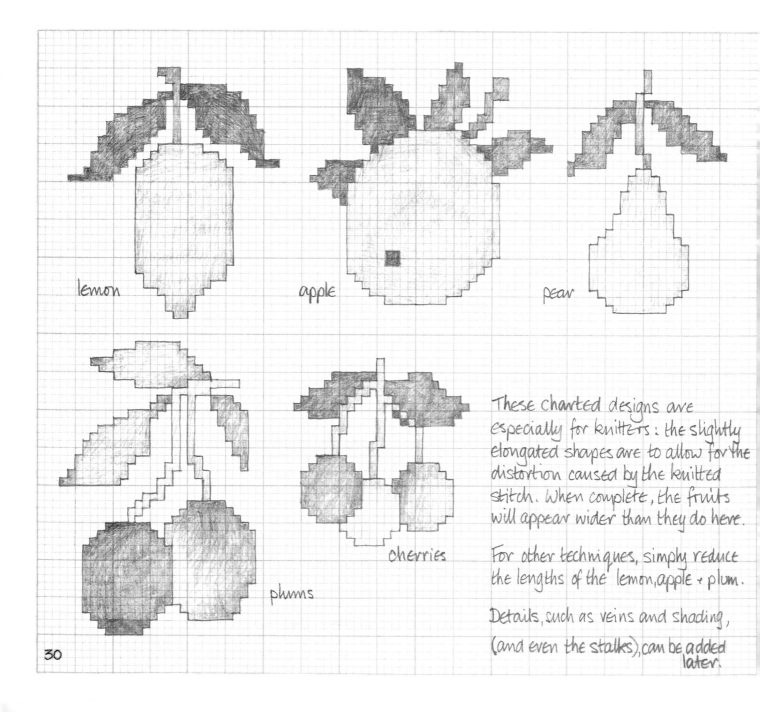

lemon

apple

pear

plums

cherries

These charted designs are especially for knitters: the slightly elongated shapes are to allow for the distortion caused by the knitted stitch. When complete, the fruits will appear wider than they do here.

For other techniques, simply reduce the lengths of the lemon, apple & plum.

Details, such as veins and shading, (and even the stalks), can be added later.

Cypress Tree motifs from 17th C. Persian textiles.

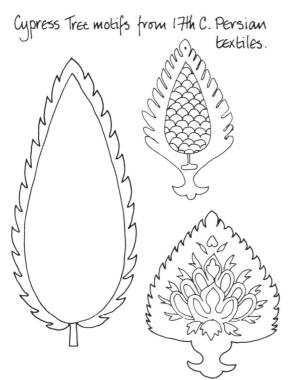

Oak leaf appliqué and quilting pattern.

Oak leaf and acorn pattern from a 14th century tile.

Notice how similar are these designs to each other.

Below: a detail from a small canvaswork cushion-cover of the 16th century, at Hardwick Hall, Derbyshire. A delightful pattern of oak leaves, each one similar to, but slightly different from the other.

The oak leaf symbolises long life and strength.

The Boteh

Also known as the Kashmir, Serabend or almond motif, but by many other names too.

Has been described as a drop of water, a fern-frond, a pear, an almond, a fig or pine-cone. It is so ancient that no-one is sure of its origin, but is thought to be linked to the shape of a cypress tree which symbolises eternal life. Has been used for centuries on the carpets and rugs of India and Persia, but in 1805 was adopted by the silk industry of Paisley in Scotland when the production of Indian-style shawls began. It then became known in Europe as "the Paisley pattern".

Depending on the area of production and on the materials used, its style ranges from almost abstract to geometric, to a mass of flowing and swirling details.

Boteh motif

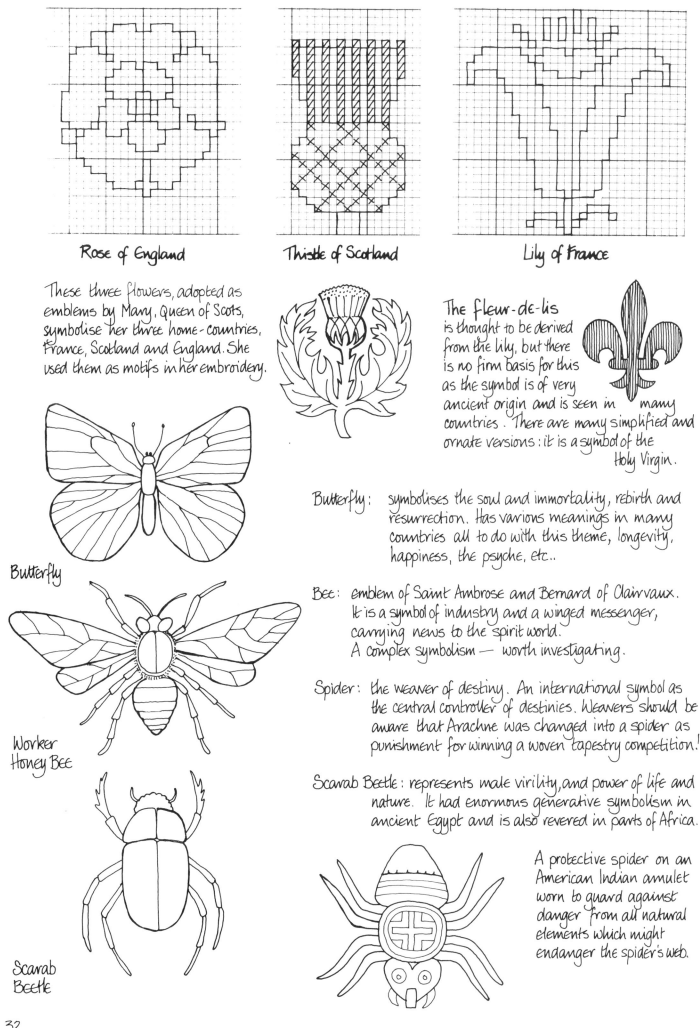

Rose of England

Thistle of Scotland

Lily of France

These three flowers, adopted as emblems by Mary, Queen of Scots, symbolise her three home-countries, France, Scotland and England. She used them as motifs in her embroidery.

The fleur-de-lis is thought to be derived from the lily, but there is no firm basis for this as the symbol is of very ancient origin and is seen in many countries. There are many simplified and ornate versions: it is a symbol of the Holy Virgin.

Butterfly

Butterfly: symbolises the soul and immortality, rebirth and resurrection. Has various meanings in many countries all to do with this theme, longevity, happiness, the psyche, etc..

Worker Honey Bee

Bee: emblem of Saint Ambrose and Bernard of Clairvaux. It is a symbol of industry and a winged messenger, carrying news to the spirit world. A complex symbolism — worth investigating.

Spider: the weaver of destiny. An international symbol as the central controller of destinies. Weavers should be aware that Arachne was changed into a spider as punishment for winning a woven tapestry competition!

Scarab Beetle: represents male virility, and power of life and nature. It had enormous generative symbolism in ancient Egypt and is also revered in parts of Africa.

Scarab Beetle

A protective spider on an American Indian amulet worn to guard against danger from all natural elements which might endanger the spider's web.

Birds

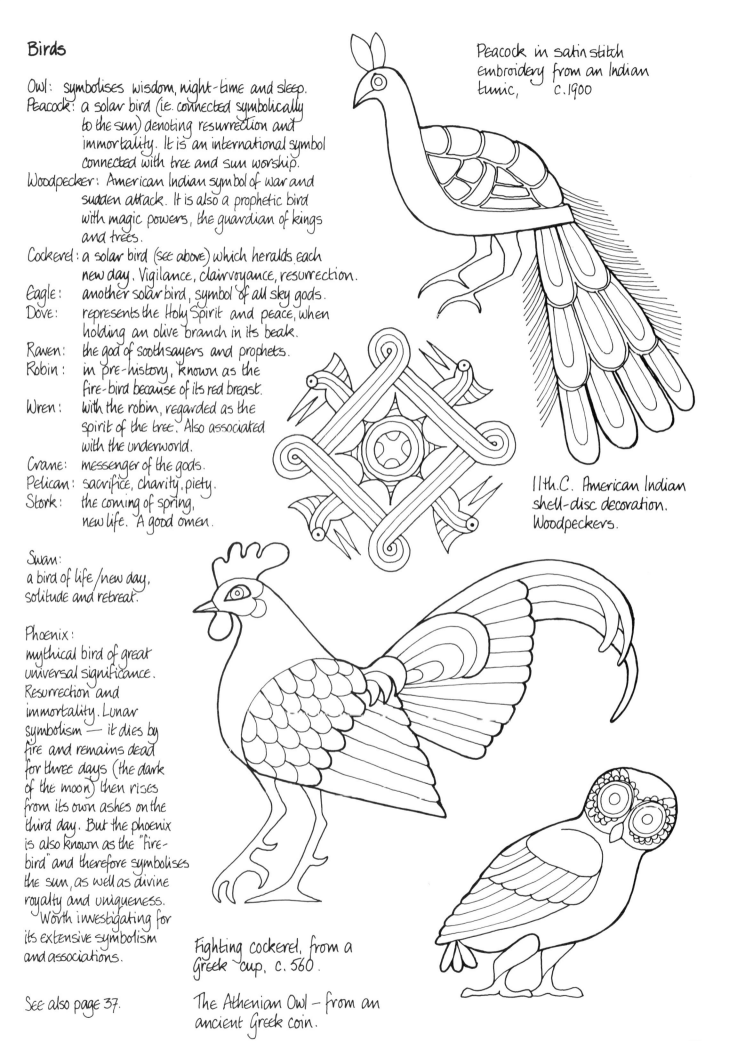

Owl: symbolises wisdom, night-time and sleep.

Peacock: a solar bird (i.e. connected symbolically to the sun) denoting resurrection and immortality. It is an international symbol connected with tree and sun worship.

Woodpecker: American Indian symbol of war and sudden attack. It is also a prophetic bird with magic powers, the guardian of kings and trees.

Cockerel: a solar bird (see above) which heralds each new day. Vigilance, clairvoyance, resurrection.

Eagle: another solar bird, symbol of all sky gods.

Dove: represents the Holy Spirit and peace, when holding an olive branch in its beak.

Raven: the god of soothsayers and prophets.

Robin: in pre-history, known as the fire-bird because of its red breast.

Wren: with the robin, regarded as the spirit of the tree. Also associated with the underworld.

Crane: messenger of the gods.

Pelican: sacrifice, charity, piety.

Stork: the coming of spring, new life. A good omen.

Swan:
a bird of life/new day, solitude and retreat.

Phoenix:
mythical bird of great universal significance. Resurrection and immortality. Lunar symbolism — it dies by fire and remains dead for three days (the dark of the moon) then rises from its own ashes on the third day. But the phoenix is also known as the "fire-bird" and therefore symbolises the sun, as well as divine royalty and uniqueness.
    Worth investigating for its extensive symbolism and associations.

See also page 37.

Peacock in satin stitch embroidery from an Indian tunic, c.1900

11th.C. American Indian shell-disc decoration. Woodpeckers.

Fighting cockerel, from a Greek cup, c. 560.

The Athenian Owl — from an ancient Greek coin.

White Hart: emblem of King Richard II (1367 - 1400)

The Eastern Dragon

stylised flames surround head

Scales cover whole of body and legs.

Ribbons spring from all four legs.

Symbols of the Evangelists

Winged Bull : St. Luke

Winged Lion : St. Mark

Winged Eagle : St. John

Lamb of God, or Agnus Dei with

Banner of Victory

Heraldic Lion

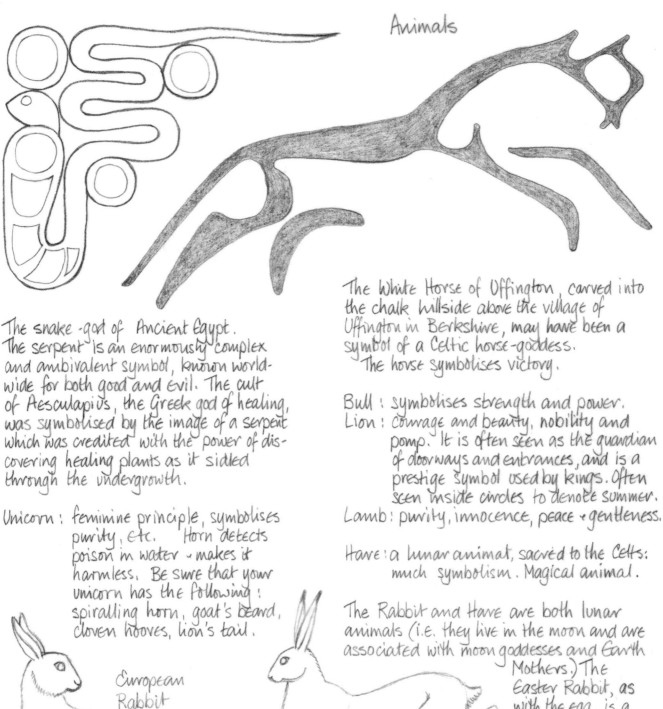

The snake-god of Ancient Egypt. The serpent is an enormously complex and ambivalent symbol, known world-wide for both good and evil. The cult of Aesculapius, the Greek god of healing, was symbolised by the image of a serpent which was credited with the power of discovering healing plants as it sidled through the undergrowth.

Unicorn: feminine principle, symbolises purity, etc. Horn detects poison in water - makes it harmless. Be sure that your unicorn has the following: spiralling horn, goat's beard, cloven hooves, lion's tail.

The White Horse of Uffington, carved into the chalk hillside above the village of Uffington in Berkshire, may have been a symbol of a Celtic horse-goddess. The horse symbolises victory.

Bull: symbolises strength and power.
Lion: courage and beauty, nobility and pomp. It is often seen as the guardian of doorways and entrances, and is a prestige symbol used by kings. Often seen inside circles to denote summer.
Lamb: purity, innocence, peace & gentleness.

Hare: a lunar animal, sacred to the Celts: much symbolism. Magical animal.

The Rabbit and Hare are both lunar animals (i.e. they live in the moon and are associated with moon goddesses and Earth Mothers.) The Easter Rabbit, as with the egg, is a pre-Christian symbol of rebirth and renewal of life at the beginning of the Vernal Equinox.

European Rabbit

European Hare.

The Rabbit is also the emblem of Eastre, Teutonic goddess of spring and dawn, and this may indicate the origin of the term 'Easter'.

The Cat is another lunar animal: its symbolism varies widely (some not so favourable), but the best bits are its attributes of stealth, desire and liberty, peace, repose and its powers of transformation. It also has psychic powers and has been revered in many civilizations.

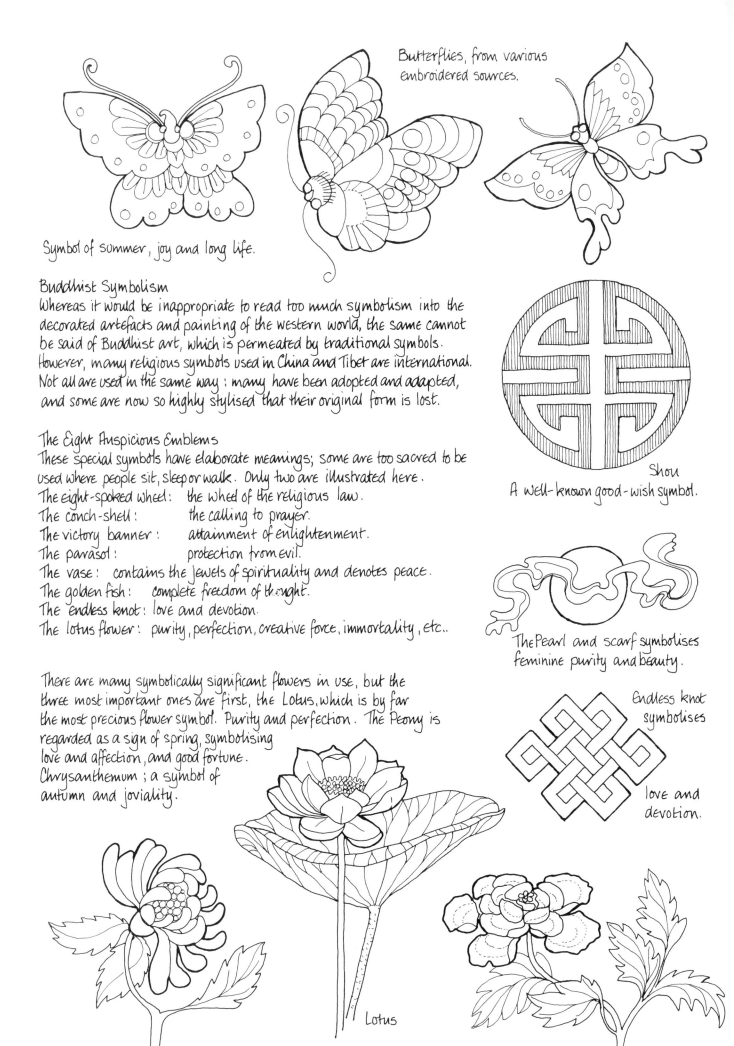

Butterflies, from various embroidered sources.

Symbol of summer, joy and long life.

Buddhist Symbolism

Whereas it would be inappropriate to read too much symbolism into the decorated artefacts and painting of the western world, the same cannot be said of Buddhist art, which is permeated by traditional symbols. However, many religious symbols used in China and Tibet are international. Not all are used in the same way : many have been adopted and adapted, and some are now so highly stylised that their original form is lost.

The Eight Auspicious Emblems

These special symbols have elaborate meanings; some are too sacred to be used where people sit, sleep or walk. Only two are illustrated here.

The eight-spoked wheel: the wheel of the religious law.
The conch-shell: the calling to prayer.
The victory banner : attainment of enlightenment.
The parasol: protection from evil.
The vase: contains the jewels of spirituality and denotes peace.
The golden fish: complete freedom of thought.
The endless knot: love and devotion.
The lotus flower : purity, perfection, creative force, immortality, etc..

There are many symbolically significant flowers in use, but the three most important ones are first, the Lotus, which is by far the most precious flower symbol. Purity and perfection. The Peony is regarded as a sign of spring, symbolising love and affection, and good fortune. Chrysanthemum ; a symbol of autumn and joviality.

Shou
A well-known good-wish symbol.

The Pearl and scarf symbolises feminine purity and beauty.

Endless knot symbolises

love and devotion.

Chrysanthemum

Lotus

Peony

Crane

Bat : detail from a mandarin's square.

The Chinese word for bat "fu" also means happiness, therefore the bat is used to symbolise happiness and good fortune.

Pheasant

These two birds both symbolise longevity.

Cockerel

Embroidery on an 18th C. emperor's robe.

Bat

Embroidered detail from a Chinese mandarin's square.

Mandarin square — these are square or round embroidered panels, two of the same design, one of which was sewn to the back of the waistcoat, and the other (divided into two halves) to either side of the front opening.

Mandarin Ducks are a symbol of conjugal happiness!

Mandarin Ducks : detail from a silk tapestry.

Chinese, late Ming dynasty (1600–1650) Metropolitan Museum of Art, New York.

SOL   ANNVS   LUNA

Above: part of a mosaic pavement in the Italian cathedral of Aosta. The Year holds the sun in his right hand and the moon in his left. Surrounding him (not shown) are twelve smaller circles containing the Labours of the Months, and the rectangle which encloses this has the four Rivers of Paradise in the corners.

Left: a simplified diagram of the roundels which form the centre of the design found in the Great Pavement of Westminster Abbey. It marks the place upon which the monarch is anointed with holy oil during the Coronation ceremony.

It symbolises the four Elements: the complex geometric patterns of coloured stone and marble seen both inside and surrounding this device add much more in the way of religious symbolism.

(See also page 19.)

Colours

Black/White represents the negative/positive, and all opposites, for example death and life, war and peace, darkness and light.

 Black: death, despair, shame, grief, etc.,
time, chaos, mourning, witchcraft, hell, winter

White: light, sun, air, purity, innocence, chastity, holiness, joy, etc.,
birth, puberty, confirmation

Red: masculine, sun, war, royalty, love, joy, energy, fire, blood,
health, anger, catastrophe, passion, fertility, evil

Blue: authority, spirituality, intellect, truth, sincerity, serenity, peace,
coolness, depth, water, sky, heaven

Green: life and death, nature, growth, regeneration, hope, eternal life,
resurrection, Spring, prosperity, peace, jealousy

Yellow: sun, life, truth, wisdom and learning, in the West — spiritual
enlightenment; treachery, betrayal, secrecy, avarice

Orange: fire, flames, humility, love and happiness, warmth

Violet: intelligence, knowledge, sorrow, nostalgia, mourning and grief,
old age, penitence

Purple: royalty, pomp, pride, justice, temperance

Brown: earth, spiritual death, renunciation, penitence

 Grey: neutral, mourning, depression, humility, anonymity

Silver: moon, feminine principle, virginity

Gold: sun, enlightenment, divine power, immortality, radiance,
glory, masculine principle

The symbolism of colour is very complex, full of contradictions and ambiguities. Over thousands of years, these accumulated meanings have been passed on from all parts of the world. Understandably, they differ, depending on the religion, culture, socio-economic structure and other regional factors. In spite of these differences, though, there is no doubt that in all of us a psychological reaction to certain colours exists which depends on personal elements which link them to past memories. This should be acknowledged in our use of colour symbolism. When all is said and done, the above list merely tells you what certain colours have meant to people in the past, not necessarily how you can use them in the future.
The boxes are for you to colour in paint or coloured pencils.

Bibliography

1. An Illustrated Encyclopaedia of Traditional Symbols.
   J.C.Cooper   (Thames and Hudson)   ISBN 0 500 27152 9

2. Christian Symbols Ancient and Modern
   Heather Child and Dorothy Colles   (Bell. London. 1971)

3. Jewish Ceremonial Embroidery
   Kathryn Salomon (Batsford)   ISBN 07134 5268 4 (£17.95)

4. Hall's Dictionary of Subjects and Symbols in Art
   (John Murray : reprinted 1985)   ISBN 0 7195 2984 0 (hardback)
                                             07195 4147 6 (paperback)

5. Heraldry for Embroiderers
   Lugg and Willcocks   (Batsford)   ISBN 0 7134 6367 8

6. Love and Marriage
   Christine Bloxham and Molly Picken (Webb & Bower, 1990)
                                    ISBN 0 86350 336 5

7. Church Furnishings / A Nadfas Guide.
   Patricia Dirsztay   (Routledge and Kegan Paul, London 1978)
                                    ISBN 07100 88205 (hardback)
                                          07100 88973 (paperback)

8. Embroidered Textiles / Traditional Patterns from Five Continents
   Sheila Paine   (Thames and Hudson, 1990)
                                    ISBN 0 500 23597 X

9. Mandarin Squares
   Valerie M.Garrett (Oxford University Press) £6.95

10. Patterns of Thought / The Hidden Meaning of the Great Pavement of
                                    Westminster Abbey.
    Richard Foster (Johnathan Cape, 1991) £15.99.
                                    ISBN 0 224 02910 X

Opposite: a fountain at Cliveden, Bucks.
            A jet of water issuing from a mouth is a symbol of the power of speech,
            instruction and refreshment.

            Sunflower: in Chinese symbolism it has magical powers and represents
            longevity. Its meaning in the western world has to do with sun-worship,
            as with the Greek Clytie who loved the sun god Apollo and
            was turned into a sunflower.

            Chrysanthemums, in Japan, signify longevity and happiness.
            It is Japan's flower emblem.